Stormy

By Alice K. Flanagan

See the light flash across the dark sky. It is lightning! Hear the boom. It is thunder!

Lightning flashes over a field.

Lightning is very bright. But it is very thin, too.

Lightning looks like a **streak** of light in the sky. It is very bright. But it is only about one inch (2.54 cm) wide.

Lightning can look like a **jagged** fork that reaches the ground. It can also be just a flash in the clouds.

Lightning can stretch from the clouds to the ground.

Sometimes lightning stays in the sky.

Lightning stays in the sky or touches the ground. Around the world, lightning touches the ground about 100 times each second.

Lightning is a burst of **electricity**. Have you ever had a **shock** after shuffling your feet on some carpet? If so, you have felt electricity. But it was only a very small amount.

Lightning can strike at any time of day or night.

Lightning strikes near a neighborhood.

Lightning heats the air around it. The hot air explodes! This causes a loud sound. That sound is thunder.

Thunder has many sounds. It can sound like a rumble or a crackle. It can sound like a loud clap.

Thunder is loud if lightning is nearby.

Lightning can strike bodies of water.

You see lightning before you hear thunder. Both sound and light travel through the air. But light travels faster. It reaches your eyes before sound reaches your ears.

In a thunder and lightning storm, stay away from tall trees and telephone poles. Lightning usually touches tall things before it travels to the ground.

Lightning moves toward a tree.

During a storm, stay indoors.

Watching lightning and listening to thunder can be fun. But make sure you do it in a safe place!

Glossary

electricity (ih-lek-TRISS-uh-tee): Electricity is a form of energy. Lightning is a burst of electricity.

jagged (JAG-id): If something is jagged, it is uneven. Lightning is usually jagged.

shock (SHOK): A shock is a spark that you feel when electricity passes through your body. A shock that comes from lightning can be harmful.

streak (STREEK): A streak is a long, thin line. Lightning often looks like a streak in the sky.

To Find Out More

Books

Goin, Miriam Busch. *Storms.* Washington, DC: National Geographic, 2009.

Jensen, Belinda. *A Party for Clouds: Thunderstorms.* Minneapolis, MN: Millbrook Press, 2016.

Rattini, Kristin Baird. *Weather*. Washington, DC: National Geographic, 2013.

Websites

Visit our website for links about stormy weather:
childsworld.com/links

Note to Parents, Teachers, and Librarians: We routinely verify our Web links to make sure they are safe and active sites. So encourage your readers to check them out!

Index

About the Author

Alice K. Flanagan lives with her husband in Chicago, Illinois, and writes books for children and teachers. Today, she has more than 70 books published on a wide variety of topics, from U.S. presidents to the weather.

The Child's World®
childsworld.com

Published by The Child's World®
1980 Lookout Drive • Mankato, MN 56003-1705
800-599-READ • www.childsworld.com

Photo credits: DrawingWithLight/Shutterstock.com: 8; DR-images/Shutterstock.com: 4; Irina Kozorog/Shutterstock.com: 20; John D Sirlin/Shutterstock.com: 3, 11; John Panella/Shutterstock.com: 12; Kanakorn/Shutterstock.com: 19; laurie schaerer/Shutterstock.com: 15; MonoLiza/Shutterstock.com: cover, 1; Nyrok555/Shutterstock.com: 7; Svet_Feo/Shutterstock.com; 16

ISBN Hardcover: 9781503827912
ISBN Paperback: 9781622434596
LCCN: 2018939778

Printed in the United States of America • PA02398